Matthew's Very Happy Day

Sally Brenden

Photography by Tim Nelson

To
Matthew
&
Uncle Bim

May God bless you with many more very happy days!

Matthew was spending the day with Uncle Bim.

What a very happy day.

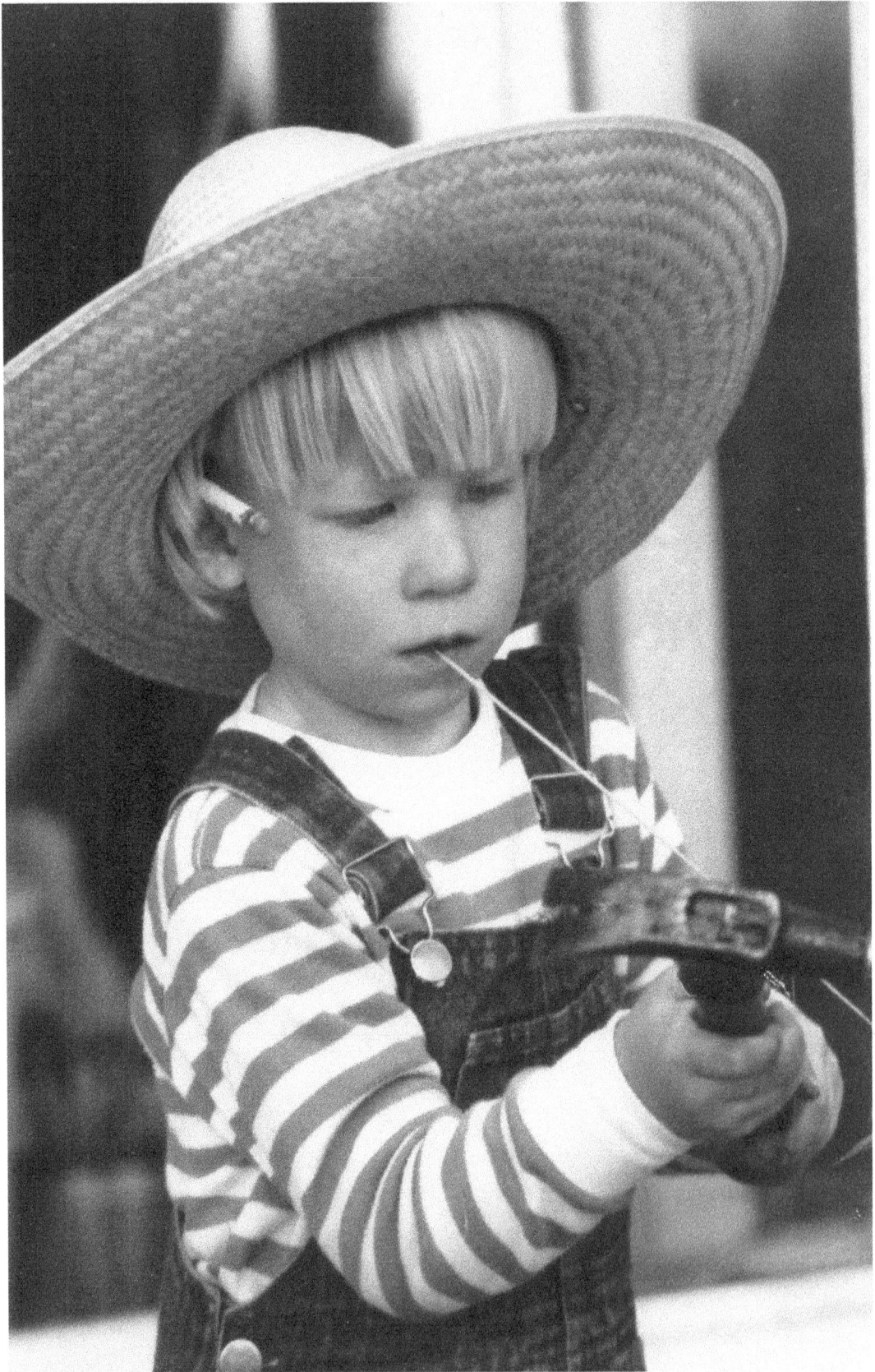

"We are making you a playhouse!" said Uncle Bim with a big smile.

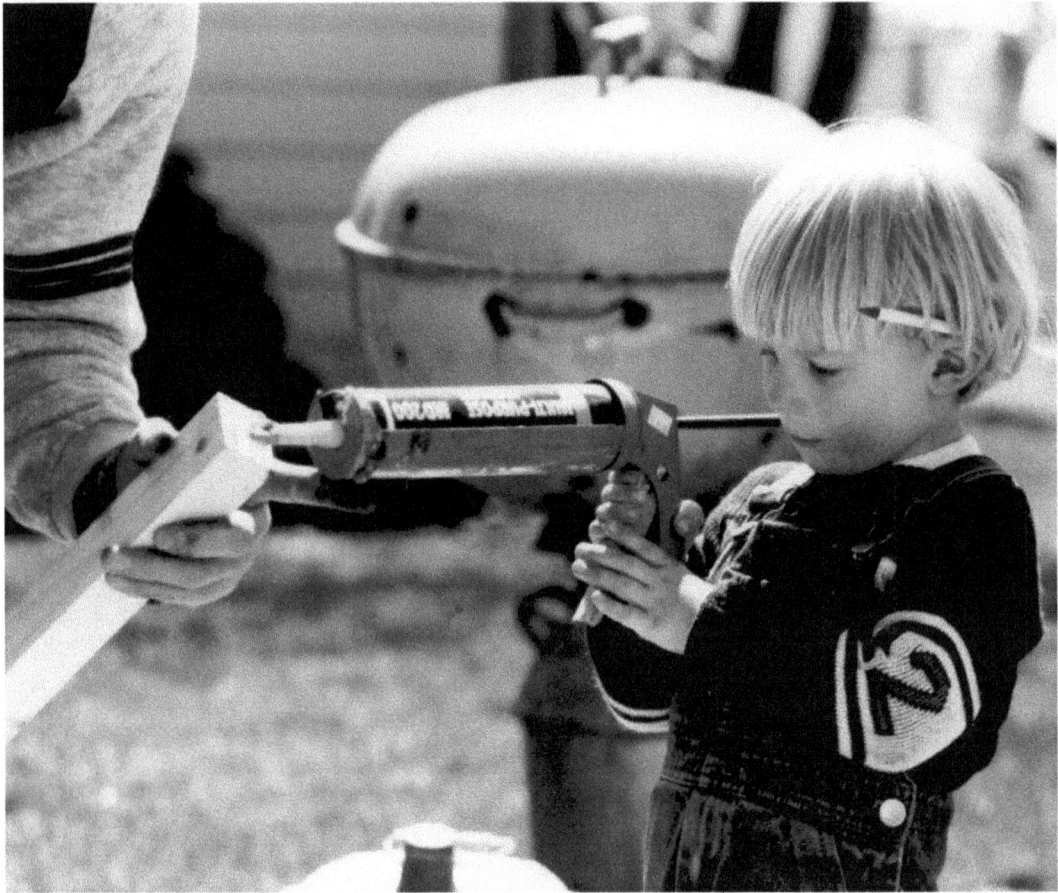

"Be careful," warned Uncle Bim.

Matthew was careful indeed.

Matthew put a piece of grass in his mouth like Uncle Bim so he could work harder.

Uncle Bim even let him pound a nail in his new playhouse.

"We menfolk work hard," said Matthew. "I'm just starving!"

Matthew thanked Jesus for the waffles and then he chowed down.

"There is no time for a nap today, Little Helper," announced Uncle Bim. "No siree!"

Happy Matthew.

Favorite Uncle Bim.

The plants in Uncle Bim's greenhouse needed watering.

"Oh-Oh!"

Off he went to the
fancy pump.

"This takes muscles,
doesn't it Uncle Bim?"

Such fun!

Such a good little helper!

Time to work in the garden now.

Matthew loved helping Uncle Bim with his big garden.

He pushed the tiller all
by himself.

He hoed.

He planted.

"Hop in if you want a ride to the mulch pile!" laughed Uncle Bim.

"Looks like you lost your hat! Is it under the leaves?" teased Uncle Bim.

It was Matthew's turn to laugh.

Silly Uncle Bim.

While Uncle Bim finished planting, Matthew hauled dirt in his little wheelbarrow.

"Look what I found
Uncle Bim!"

Uncle Bim stopped working.

"I guess this means we have to go fishing!"

Matthew thought that was a wonderful idea.

Off to the river they went.

"Any luck?" asked
Uncle Bim.

"Nothing biting yet,"
answered Matthew.

"Maybe they will if I sit down."

If a fish bit we will never know because soon Uncle Bim's little helper was snoozing.

What a very happy day!

www.ingramcontent.com/pod-product-compliance
Lightning Source LLC
Chambersburg PA
CBHW080535030426
42337CB00023B/4747